Roger Federer

A Biography of the Tennis Legend

BENJAMIN SOUTHERLAND

Visit Benjamin Southerland's website at
benjaminsoutherland.com.

ISBN: 1522904328
ISBN-13: 978-1522904328

Table of Contents

Chapter 1: An Introduction to the Legacy of Roger Federer

The greatness of prolific athletes cannot be defined by just one aspect of their lives, not solely by their career accomplishments, nor by their notoriety and celebrity status. The judgment of the prolific athlete lies within the all-encompassing body of work they were able to compile during the extent of their careers. Whether they dominated their competition or compiled otherworldly statistics, there are a variety of measuring sticks used to evaluate a celebrity-athlete's impact upon the world which has revered them for their talents.

Roger Federer, the Swiss-born tennis legend, has become one of the most well-rounded and professionally accomplished humans in the history of sport. As a whole, the sporting world watches closely as talented athletes vie for victory on a public platform and engage in competitive battle for all to admire. Federer embodied the spirit of the "alpha-dog," just as fellow "alphas" like Tiger Woods and Michael Jordan similarly have. Not a single part of Federer's career is underwhelming or anti-climactic. From the tumultuous rivalries to utter domination of his sport, Federer lives up to the designation so many professional athletes chase but never quite achieve: Legend.

Because of the fact he was born in Europe, he inherently faced the challenge of becoming an international star, particularly in America, where tennis has thrived but is not overtly popular. Federer's stardom eventually soared within the States as well as abroad, and he defined what tennis (specifically men's tennis) meant for an entire generation of fans. In fact, the challenge he was presented with in trying to become a star, both internationally and in America, actually makes his rise to becoming a household name that much more incredible. Because the United States is the largest commercial market with the most active consumers, foreign stars often seek to find the most lucrative marketing opportunities there.

The difficult nature of this fulfillment is on display frequently, as in the case of Lionel Messi, who is hugely popular but has not entirely caught on as a national brand within the United States, despite being widely recognized as soccer's most recognizable modern star. Federer was able to transcend this threshold, which almost certainly adds to his legacy as an extremely well-known athlete. He went on to become a popular and frequently employed spokesperson for several huge brands, including American companies—something that very few international stars are able to harness with the United States. In fact, one could argue Federer has set the bar very high for all other foreign-born stars to aspire to reach, as far as brand recognition goes.

One of the most significant aspects of his career is the fact that he has the numbers to reinforce a legitimate claim as the greatest ever to play *his* game. It is not simply as if he shares many all-time records with several other players; he *specifically* owns the record for most all-time Grand Slams, often considered to be the ultimate measure of a tennis player's significance.

Chapter 2: Discovering a First Love in Tennis

Federer was born to parents from different cultural backgrounds. His father, Robert, was Swiss and his mother, Lynette, South African. He grew up in an area of Switzerland known for being at the intersection of the Swiss, French, and German borders: the city of Basel, a moderately sized city known for its industrial and manufacturing background. The city is also recognized for its blend of religious and cultural backgrounds. A climate of extraordinary diversity has led to generations of multi-lingual citizens of this region. Federer himself speaks three languages. In fact, he actually displayed an ability to develop fluency in more than just spoken word.

The theory of 10,000 hours, which dictates that one must exceed 10,000 hours of practice at a particular craft in order to excel at it, was originated by Malcolm Gladwell.

Federer benefited from a great education as a child. He was born in Basel, Switzerland but was eventually raised in several places. These included Birsfelden and Riehen when he was younger, followed by Munchenstein, an area with a more intensive athletic focus. Federer began to gravitate toward tennis as his primary focus when he reached double digits in age, but like most famous athletes in the historical sports landscape, he did play a wide variety of sports from an early age. Kobe Bryant was playing basketball against adults in Europe when he was a pre-teen. Tiger Woods was an excellent child-athlete which led to his utterly dominant run as a golf pro (similar to Federer's eventual reign in tennis). Like Federer, Woods pursued the legends of his own sport like Jack Nicklaus and Arnold Palmer, as well as a fierce rival in Phil Mickelson and a host of other challengers. The parallels between these two athletes are evident and apparent in the grand scheme of each of their careers.

Kobe Bryant similarly went on to pursue the legend of those who came before him. Whether it was his predecessors with the Los Angeles Lakers or other NBA greats, Bryant was another child athlete who was competitive as a youth and went on to pursue greatness.

Many professional athletes excelled at a variety of sports while they were young, but some do not necessarily follow that path. Interestingly, however, the common theme among the all-time greats of any sport is the exceptional athleticism at an early age. Coordination, balance, and other sorts of skills developed at an early age always seem to play a role in the child-prodigy turning into an all-time great at the fruition of their career.

Federer's personal idol in tennis was Boris Becker, whom he watched perform as a child growing up in the 1980s. He credits Becker with being an influence on his style and for igniting some of the personal passion he developed for the sport, first as a fan and then as a participant in the sport of tennis. One of the most interesting examinations of the anatomy of star athletes is who they idolized, discovering which people had the greatest impact upon their lives other than an individual's parents. Defining which other person helped to shape some of their initial aspirations toward a particular topic or pursuit is instrumental in discovering what makes an athlete's internal clock "tick". Interestingly, Becker compares with Federer because of his one-time ranking as world's number one male tennis player and the fact that he won six majors in his career. Although Federer eventually went on to supersede Becker's personal accomplishments, it is worth noting that he once looked up to a particular player.

Federer entered the world of tennis for the first time at the age of six. He reportedly became the best player in his age group immediately during his first venture into the sport as a youth. He excelled above the rest of his peers and developed into a force within the Swiss youth tennis environment. In 1995, Roger was accepted by the Swiss Tennis development program for young people in Switzerland hoping to become professional tennis players. Federer has described it as a difficult transition as he moved away from home for the first time at the age of 14. Leaving his hometown, he began the first step in his journey to becoming one of the most legendary tennis players of all time and certainly the most famous Swiss athlete ever. He moved away from his family for the first time and then began his first step into his historic future.

According to Federer himself, his early entrance into tennis training was coupled with plenty of adversity. There are many stories of athletes facing difficult situations on their long journey to stardom. One of the most popular examples of this is the constantly referenced "Michael Jordan was cut by his high school basketball coach," because he was not excelling or outstanding compared with the other players on the team. The story goes that he used the adverse situation as the fuel for his burning flame of passion. He ignited his legendary career as perhaps the most famous cross-platform athlete ever as a result of his very own youth coach doubting him. Of course, his otherworldly talent contributed to his ultimate success.

Similarly, Federer has documented his early time at the national tennis academy of Eculben as very trying initially. Although he went on to excel competitively and advance his amateur career into a profession, he has described not having much of an advantage, physically, when he first began his tennis education. It was a detriment that he was among the smallest and least imposing members of his training classes. Although he is credited with being a multi-lingual speaker nowadays, Federer himself explained that his struggles with speaking French presented him with the most challenges early on in his transition process away from home. Growing up in the Basel region of Switzerland, he spoke a Swiss-German dialect. He moved throughout various suburbs of Basel as a youth, but none of these moves resulted in him having to shift his language skills to adjust. So, when he moved away, he naturally had a very difficult time with the language barrier he was faced with upon relocation. As he progressed at the academy, Federer gradually advanced along the national Swiss rankings systems. At this time, little did he know he would one day go on to become the most dominantly ranked player, internationally, ever.

An extremely interesting glimpse inside the psyche of Federer comes in 1997, when the 16-year-old made another dynamic life-changing decision. This next step is also another parallel with many other athletes who decide to make the choice of devotion to their craft. Malcolm Gladwell's theory of 10,000 hours comes in to play here as well, as do overriding themes of maturity. Themes of preparation and dedication adorn this next stepping stone in Federer's path to greatness. He made the difficult choice, considering the potential consequences of failure, to entirely devote himself to his sport. He sacrificed the continuation of his academic educational career, forsaking it for the advancement of his tennis talent. This obviously becomes the dominant driving force into his foray as a legendary tennis player. This is typically the case with many of his athletic peers who likely each had to make this same choice at some point in order to advance their physical talents as an athlete. Kobe Bryant and LeBron James famously entered the NBA Draft immediately following their high school careers and forsook a potential college education. Financial circumstances do play a part in this process as well, considering amateur players are not paid for their athletic feats.

Federer's decision was made much to the chagrin of his parents. They certainly felt uneasy about him taking the next step. Publicly, this process certainly makes sense as well, because it is obvious that a random pair of parents would believe it to be a better idea to pursue a conventional and stable life, through obtaining a solid education, rather than seeking to earn a living as a professional athlete. In all sports, the chances of reaching prosperity and sustenance via a professional sports career always point toward a highly unlikely occurrence; however, the gamble is sometimes worth the risk. After hearing from his youth coaches and others about his supreme level of talent. Federer must have felt personally confident in the decision, although any human would be slightly unsure about the decision until the fulfillment of his or her goals came to fruition.

Essentially, when a youth completes nine levels of mandatory education in Switzerland, they have the option of discontinuing their educational pursuit or advancing into a post-secondary educational career. Quite obviously, this was a hugely instrumental step in his early career; therefore it is reasonable to conclude that he may not ever have become as great of a player had he not fully dedicated himself at such an early age. His craft became tennis, and likely due to a solid education when he *was* younger, not yet a tennis prodigy, he became a well-rounded adult individual.

In 1998, Federer became the premier junior player in Switzerland. He had several important matches including one extremely notable bout with Andre Agassi, Federer's first venture into the world of cross-generational sporting comparisons. Agassi, who had become a tennis legend by the time Federer was entering into the sport, had faced his fair share of comparisons to other tennis greats. Once again, as the young Federer advanced through his early career, he would become part of the cycle of comparisons once he established himself as a legitimate force within the sport. Eventually, he became perhaps the most dominant ever, which lead to even more thorough comparisons, put on display in tangible form during his rivalries with his contemporaries as well. Sporting fans and critics, however, will always attempt to define a player's place within history, rather than simply crediting their talent in the modern era. Tennis, much like golf, is an easy sport in which to compare athletes of multiple generations. Federer's match with Agassi likely sparked these comparisons in Federer's own mind as well.

Chapter 3: Early Career and Establishment as a Title Contender

By the turn of the 21st century, Federer took the first steps toward his viability as an actual title contender in the professional realm. After going pro, a young tennis player seeking to become relevant on the international stage and within tournaments must, eventually, work their way into significant victories over capable opponents. They are certainly provided some initial leeway, but those who go on to become all-time greats typically start to obtain their signature wins quickly and then begin to rapidly advance. The tennis landscape is enormous and the sheer volume of tournaments played by professionals is vast.

Federer made his deepest advancement into a Grand Slam Major, with his 2000 performance in the Australian

Open. While he did not win, he had a good run that year, and continued to build his momentum. Federer also went on to play in his first Olympics in the first year of the new millennium, also played in "the Land Down Under." Sydney was home to the 2000 Olympics and Federer performed well, eventually losing but only after a competitive and noteworthy performance representing his homeland. The Olympics are obviously a highly cherished part of any athlete's life.

According to Federer himself, his trip to Sydney was more meaningful in another way. The notion of something becoming more important than an Olympic appearance may seem ridiculous upon first glance. However, the event which surpassed his Olympic run was meeting a fellow tennis player during his time in Sydney. Mirka Vavrinec, his future wife, was also participating in the world games, representing her home nation of Russia. They met in the Olympic village, and this event certainly shaped Roger's personal life for the rest of his life.

The next several years saw many important matches for the rising star in the tennis world; however, none was bigger at that point than his match against the legendary Pete Sampras in 2001. The American, who once-upon-a-time held the record for most Grand Slam singles victories among male tennis players, was thirty years old (ten years Federer's senior) when they faced off at

Wimbledon that year. Sampras was coming off an undeniable run of domination on the English pitch, where he had won thirty-one straight matches in London up to that point. The young challenger defeated the veteran in his most thoroughly dominated domain. Publicly, at that time, Sampras was known as the most dominant player to play at Wimbledon, and it was a crucial victory for Federer's rising young star power. Upon defeating Sampras on that day, he became internationally relevant for perhaps the first time in his life. It would ultimately serve as an extraordinarily symbolic victory as well. Since Federer one day would surpass Sampras in the all-time championship rankings, it is intriguing to revisit the outcome of their first meeting and how it became instrumental in the rise of Federer to popular heights, internationally.

That year, however, he was unable to ascend to the pinnacle of his sport, which would be a Grand Slam championship, as he lost in the next round. Nevertheless, it would serve as another crucial building block toward that final goal.

The earliest landmark achievement occurred two years later in 2003. After a thrilling run through the semifinal rounds of Wimbledon, he reached the pinnacle of a tennis player's career much sooner than many ever have a chance to taste something so cherished. Federer won the Wimbledon title for the first time against Mark

Philippoussis. For a player who would go on to eventually win the most individual titles in the history of his sport, the first major title is obviously of significant importance. As his first major victory, it began the momentum he needed in order to achieve so many more championships in the years to follow.

The following year, Federer added to his titles collection by winning three more championships. He was victorious at Wimbledon for the second consecutive year but also added wins at the Australian Open and US Open for the first time in his career. The triple-winner further accelerated his international profile as well as his ranking on the Association of Tennis Professionals (ATP) list, as he finished 2004 as the number one ranked player in the world. A lifelong dream and an incredible journey had been fulfilled at such a young age. Already an owner of four Grand Slam titles, Federer was beginning to lay the very solid foundation of his burgeoning professional tennis career. He had wholly established himself as one of the most exciting young stars in the game and was showing no signs of letting up his assault on the ATP rankings.

Much in the same way Roger once defeated a legendary player of his lifetime, he fell in 2005 to the young upstart Rafael Nadal, who was 19 years old at the time of their meeting in France. Despite this let down, it became quite evident that Nadal was a phenomenal young player and

Federer must have known, deep down, he would meet the young player many more times throughout his career. Federer still had a phenomenal season and emerged from it with two more Grand Slam victories to add to his resume at this stage; and most crucially, he successfully maintained his ranking as the number one player in the world.

During the next three years, he enjoyed what many believe to be his most successful period of dominance in his entire career. He won seven more Grand Slam titles in these next three years, and accomplished some significant feats along the way, including becoming the first player since Bjorn Borg to win a Grand Slam without conceding a single set to his opponent. This could quite possibly be the best example of his pure domination as an athlete. Not unlike a baseball pitcher tossing a shutout or a goalkeeper keeping the other team off the scoreboard, a truly overwhelming performance is evident when the opponent never even had a chance to envision victory.

In 2009, Federer won a legendarily lengthy match against Andy Roddick in the Wimbledon final, but only after already having won the French Open as well. In the same year, he married his fiancé, and she gave birth to their first set of twins. Federer was enjoying another "dream" season. Although he had some narrow escapes, particularly against Roddick in the final in London,

Federer statistically compiled another great season. His magical year continued all the way until he fell at the hands of Juan Martin del Potro in the US Open final, as many theorize his hugely action-packed year had taken too much of a toll for him to win the final major he entered.

After a 2010 season in which he won yet another major title, this time in Australia once again, Federer finally ended his reign as the world's number one, which he enjoyed for a record 286 consecutive weeks. Rafael Nadal, his bitter rival, supplanted him as number one in the world ATP rankings. The next year, Federer failed to win a Grand Slam title for the first time in the past nine years (hardly any sort of failure by any measure). He also dropped to number three in the world rankings by the end of the season.

In 2012, Federer returned to Grand Slam victory, as he won his seventh and most recent Wimbledon title. However, this time, it was a dramatically more intricate run to the final match. After meeting Novak Djokovic once again in the semi-finals, the two underwent an epic match by all accounts, truly cementing theirs as the most evenly contested rivalry of Federer's career. Although it was not the final, it has been described as one of the highlights of each of their careers, as it was a thrilling match. Interestingly, Djokovic had become the favored contender to win Wimbledon in 2012, while Federer was the underdog that time around. The match was evenly paced, but became tumultuous as each player took his turn commanding the match, with Federer eventually pulling ahead significantly and taking the win. This led to a final showdown with Andy Murray, a player Federer was quite familiar with and another fairly even rivalry, although not quite as closely contested as his series of matches against Djokovic.

As of 2015, Federer has 14 career wins and 11 losses at the hands of Murray. This close level of competition displays why this makes a legitimate case for Federer's second best rivalry, since his contests with Nadal favor Rafael in the all-time head-to-head record by a significant margin. Making the case for Djokovic and Murray as one and two, respectively, in order of best Federer rivalries, is certainly possible if the measurement is based on competitiveness. While Federer vs. Nadal was the most widely recognizable rivalry, perhaps in all of sports, it was not quite as closely contested as the other two. The media effectively boosted the legend of Federer vs. Nadal by depicting it in a multitude of contrasts. By introducing the contest as old vs. young, established vs. new and even good vs. evil, the rivalry grew to take on a life of its own. Other than Borg vs. McEnroe, considered the most popular initial, mainstream rivalry within the sphere of tennis as a sport, Federer and Nadal reached heights in the public sphere that no other match has done. It cannot be understated how much this rivalry did for the sport, especially within the United States audience.

In many respects, Roger himself has described 2013 as a wholly underwhelming year, when compared to the many accomplishments of his career. It provides a stark contrast of something disappointing for Federer when compared with the extraordinary accomplishments of his decorated career. He has done quite a lot within the sport of tennis in order to establish himself in the context of the all-time greats. Naturally, a year without a Grand Slam title proves to be most trying for Federer as he approaches his veteran seasons and surely the beginning of the twilight of his stellar career. For the first time since he ascended into the top five ATP rankings, Federer finished outside of the top circle of players, falling to seventh and eventually finishing sixth by the end of 2013. Surely, this was an absolute disappointment, but he made the best of many of his competitions during the season.

Several of his lesser competitors were dominated, and he actually started strong in each of the majors he played in, but he had a difficult time sustaining success throughout the duration of each tournament, falling to Andy Murray in the final of the Australian Open. Another disappointing loss followed in the next month as he lost to up-and-comer Tomas Berdych in Dubai. Subsequently, he fell in the quarterfinals of the French Open to a lesser opponent again. It was becoming increasingly clearer that this was not shaping up to be a particularly favorable year for Swiss legend. After falling once more in dramatically disappointing fashion at Wimbledon, Federer dropped to fifth in the ATP rankings for the first time, as he did not reach the quarterfinals level in a major for the first time in years.

After addressing some of the anti-climactic matches Federer experienced on the tennis court during 2013, a much more personally troubling problem grasped Federer around this time. After dealing with back issues as a younger man, they emerge once again later in his career in the form of spasms and occasionally severe back pain, hampering many of his 2013 performances. Those who follow Federer have come to associate his 2013 campaign with injury struggles and consider it a "lost season," in many respects.

A Tennis.com article published in 2014 revealed Federer decided to switch rackets for the first time in many years and upgrade to a larger diameter racket. He had played for many years against opponents who utilized the larger rackets, but he resisted change due to the vast multitude of successes he had enjoyed throughout the entirety of his career to this point. The year 2014 brought the hope of new fortunes to Federer; he played well to begin the year and did great work on the courts as he progressed throughout the season. He accomplished a great amount of success early on, as he played a tightly contested match with Nadal in the semi-finals of the Australian Open but eventually lost to his Spanish counterpart. Near the end of his run in 2014, he played an outstanding Wimbledon tournament and began to re-establish himself on the London court, ultimately reaching a final only to fall to Novak Djokovic in a legendary, five-set match. He was, however, able to defeat his Serbian rival in another, lesser match near the end of 2014, in China. He ended an otherwise optimistic year, on a bit of a sour note after progressing through quite a few encouraging matches; he became injured once again in his back region and faced a difficult period at the end of the year.

While 2015 presented its fair share of disappointments in the sense that he was unable to capture an additional Grand Slam title, Federer remained competitive among the world's most excellent players, including minor victories over both Andy Murray and Novak Djokovic in the same year. He finished very closely at the US open and Wimbledon, but once again, he could not quite capture total victory. For the second consecutive year, Federer fell to Djokovic in the Wimbledon final, this time in four sets. It culminated a year of near misses and frustrating patch of Federer's overall career.

Chapter 4: International Super-Stardom, Rivalries, and the Ascent of a Tennis Icon

There is one record which defines Roger Federer's tennis career and cements his place among the all-time greats of his game. His 17 Grand Slam Singles titles are the most ever won by a single tennis player. This includes seven Wimbledon titles, for each time he conquered an opponent on the hallowed British grass court. Those seven titles are tied for the all-time lead. From 2003 to 2012, Federer won each of his titles, successfully and thoroughly dominating his sport for most of his career, while still remaining wholly relevant on the front and back end of that historic run. He is also the only tennis player ever to reach ten Wimbledon titles. There may be no tennis court more internationally revered and recognized by tennis fans and common folk alike. His utter dominance of that very turf may have also played a role in the amount of exposure he received throughout his career.

However, one of the most unique qualities of Federer's career is how thoroughly fluent he was at each type of playable surface in tennis. Typically, tennis critics seek to find a weakness in a player's game based on the courts they may not have been excellent on. Whether grass, clay or hard court, Federer is the only tennis player in history to win a title on each separate type of surface. In the Open Era of tennis (since the beginning of the French Open, the US Open, Wimbledon, and the Australian Open), he is also the only player to reach 27 Grand Slam matches in the men's division. He won 17.

Another interesting aspect of Federer's career accomplishments is his stunning dominance atop the ATP rankings of tennis. The ATP stands for the Association of Tennis Professionals, and they compile the definitive ratings charts for both men's and women's tennis competitions. They annually rank the players, and throughout the year, update their rankings based on results much in the same way golf players are ranked in the PGA. The most shocking aspect of Federer's relationship with the ATP is how much he was favored throughout his career. A phenomenal record 302 weeks as the number one player in the world atop the ATP rankings is one of the most resounding aspects of his resume, second only to his record 17 Grand Slam titles, of course. Of those 302 weeks, 287 were consecutive. That is also the record for most all time. These numbers speak to the sheer volume and substance of Federer's accomplishments. It is truly stunning how effective he has been throughout his entire sporting career, and these historic accomplishments obviously display that.

Federer has had many thrilling and fantastic matches throughout his career. Many served as milestones, such as his first Grand Slam title, or his initial Wimbledon title. Some of his thrillers with Rafael Nadal, Novak Djokovic, Andy Murray, Andy Roddick, and his matches with many other tennis players have entertained the tennis world for over a decade. Many of the most epic matches of his career came in the form of milestones. The sheer fact that he was able to surpass the initial world record of 14 Grand Slam titles, held by Pete Sampras, decidedly means that Federer's career has been measured and scrutinized by way of his accomplishments.

People, particularly sports fans, love to measure players and teams within the context of their predecessors. They also frequently compare the greatness of an individual based on what followed them. Just as Federer was compared with the tennis legends he once surpassed on the list of career accomplishments, he will one day be measured against the advancements of a future generation of great players. Rafael Nadal, at five years Federer's junior, may still have time to add to his 14 Grand Slam titles before his career begins to run out of steam. Additionally, Novak Djokovic has had an enormous impact upon the game as well. At the tender age of 28, he has already won ten titles of his own, and has plenty of time to add to his legacy. Although it certainly does become more difficult, as history has shown, to win titles as a tennis player ages. There are many other players who represent the present and future of tennis, but none has had the startling career of Federer up to this point.

One of the most significant components of Roger Federer's career has become the concept of rivalries as a part of his legacy. His most famous is absolutely with Nadal, while his most competitive and evenly matched rival has been Djokovic. Of the many other established rivalries present throughout his career, his matches with Djokovic and Andy Murray stand as the most closely contested. Roger leads Djokovic 17 to 16 in their all-time matches against one another, while he also has a slight edge against Murray at 14 to 11. Among other notably great players with whom he has had a substantial rivalry, Federer has significantly dominated the match-ups. This is most evident against the American Andy Roddick, who he has absolutely dominated throughout the course of their respective careers. Andre Agassi, who was not truly in his prime when he faced off against the Swiss champion, was also convincingly mastered in their 11 times prior to Agassi's eventual retirement.

Stunningly, Rafael Nadal, the man who once defeated Federer for the first time as a 19-year-old holds the only favorable record against Federer out of those who have played him more than one time. Their rivalry resulted in Nadal holding a 23–11 advantage over Federer all-time. This is not stunning from the perspective that Nadal is a great player and phenomenal talent, but this is unique because he is the one player who essentially "had Federer's number" throughout their career match-ups. If Roger Federer was asked to provide his honest opinion regarding his rivalry with Nadal, it is unclear what his answer would be. There are two definitive sides to this argument. The first possible reaction would be that Federer would have liked to sustain his dominance over everyone he ever had a substantial rivalry with, rather than have a losing record against Nadal. However, the second option is more reflective. The idea that his rivalry with Nadal may have helped to enhance his own brand by way of showing the world that he had an interesting rival—one who could make the match-ups truly interesting. Because of the fact that he finally had a "true" rival, who actually has beaten him more times than he, himself, has been victorious. They are both quite "victorious" in the end, however, because the rivalry goes down in history as one of the most viewed and anticipated battles of sports history. The knowledgeable perspective on this topic likely concludes that Federer would be quite pleased with his relationship to Nadal, if only because it is cemented as perhaps the greatest rivalry in tennis history. If not, it is certainly a close second to Bjorn Borg and John McEnroe, the concept of which really sparked the idea of "rivalry" in tennis and definitely pushed the idea of tennis as a fierce competition into the forefront of its spectators' minds. After Borg vs. McEnroe, tennis was able to lay legitimate claim to its capability as a ferociously competitive sport, establishing it as supremely captivating television. What Borg vs. McEnroe was able to do for the introduction of dramatic tennis theater as a spectator sport, Federer vs. Nadal was able to crystallize what "rivalry" meant to the sport. Ultimately, it would make a great deal of sense for Federer to be happy about the rivalry he has enjoyed with Nadal. Utter dominance of his peers, while entirely impressive, is not nearly as intriguing as a closely contested rivalry. While it may sound sacrilegious to even suggest the very notion, it is true. The viewing public is most definitely more captivated by an intense and heated rivalry rather than a one-sided affair.

By the time he established himself as one of the greatest to ever play the game, analysts began to disseminate his style of play from the other greats of the game. His fastest recorded serve of an incredible 137 mph is roundly complemented by his versatile playing style, earning high praise from many of the game's legends and many analysts of the sport.

During the height of his dominance and prominence as an international sporting megastar, Federer was able to obtain many lucrative sponsorship deals with various companies. The development of his brand from tennis player to great tennis player, to multiple Grand Slam champion was equaled only by his development as a household name, both internationally and in the United States. He has become the highest earning tennis player ever, thanks to his many sponsorship deals as well as his career earnings from the sport itself. However, the true substance of his fortune has come his way as a result of the fantastic business opportunities he was able to secure. Among his most notable sponsorship deals include partnerships with Nike, Gillette, Rolex, Mercedes-Benz, Credit Suisse, and Wilson (the tennis and athletic gear company). He earns an incredibly substantial living as the face of these companies' marketing campaigns in many cases. He gained a particularly notable amount of exposure due to his Gillette advertisements on television.

In 2015, Roger Federer was ranked number 16 on the Forbes top 100 earning celebrities when he hauled in a whopping $67 million. According to Forbes, the breakdown of his earnings paints the picture perfectly.

Federer earned $9 million from his tennis earnings alone in 2015, while an enormous $58 million was earned through his sponsorship compensation. From a financial standpoint, within the context of Federer's career as a brand and earner, he stands alone atop lifetime prize money earnings within tennis at $90 million for his career. Strictly from tournaments and prize winnings alone, he earned that substantial amount. Forbes also has reported that Federer earns approximately $40 million each year from the companies which employ him as a brand ambassador and representative. The focus on his earning power as an international brand is central to the analysis of how prominent Federer has become as a public figure—not only as an extremely recognizable athlete, but also as a true celebrity with extraordinary international prominence. He has parlayed this level of public recognition into a net worth reportedly north of $300 million.

Roger Federer has become one of the most decorated and accomplished athletes of any generation. Setting aside for a moment the utter dominance of his generation of tennis peers, Federer ranks among the all-time most awarded athletes in the history of human sport. Whether it is a team sport or individual sport, Federer ranks as one of the most accomplished athletes, as well as one of the most recognizable brands in the world. The list of products he has endorsed is long and filled with major, international companies.

For an entire generation of fans, Roger Federer symbolized true artistry at the top of his game. An American child, for example represented one of the most captive audiences Federer could have ever played in front of. Generations of Swiss children certainly idolized Federer, the most prominent Swiss athlete in the modern era and perhaps all time. However, modern sports and the ascension of their popularity can best be measured by the sheer number of people who are able to view the sporting event. The United States has represented the largest television audience in the modern world, since the Mid-20th century. In the 1950s, American homes and families began purchasing televisions at an exorbitant rate, and the amount of televisions per household has only increased exponentially in the years to follow. Hundreds of millions of modern Americans have been raised with a taste for theater, drama, and competition in various forms. Sporting events have presented a modern form of drama incomparable to its predecessors, such as stage and musical performances. There is a thirst for sports in America unlike any other public calling, particularly among the youth. While soccer is huge in Europe, hockey dominates Canada, and American Football is currently the reigning champion in the U.S., the multi-cultural blend of nationalities has inspired a diversified sporting landscape even in the case of tennis, where public popularity is modest, but large events like the U.S. Open can captivate many in the U.S. Tennis has had a dedicated following of older fans raised on the John McEnroe generation of tennis, but Roger Federer and Rafael Nadal helped bring another generation of sports fans to the spectating realm of tennis.

Prior to their much publicized rivalry, millions of school children played tennis in middle school and high school, and found a natural attraction to it, likely inspired by their parents and encouraged to try the sport as an alternative to other solo sports or perhaps as a contrast to team sports such as football, baseball, or basketball. However, in the United States, there is always an entirely additional partition of a sports audience to be captured simply through spectating. Many tennis fans in the United States likely play tennis as well. The type of sporting audiences found in America find plenty of joy and enthusiasm in the pure drama of sport. The lure of competitive battle between two teams or two separate individuals has attracted millions of fans for decades.

In the 1970s and 1980s, basketball exploded because the national audience was captivated by Larry Bird and his Celtics clashing with Magic Johnson's Lakers. The two teams were from different worlds within the same country. The Celtics hailed from traditionalist Boston while the Lakers played their home games in flashy Los

Angeles. It was the perfect sort of contrast the NBA needed to draw in an entire generation of fans. The Pittsburgh Steelers and Oakland Raiders inspired the concept of competitive rivalry within the dramatic landscape of the NFL, boosting its popularity among modern fans.

Federer vs. Nadal captivated American youth and young to middle-aged adults, alike. This was due to the intense rivalry found in this match-up. America found a reason to root. It had the perfect blend of characteristics found present in any major sports rivalry which was able to captivate a large audience. First, it had the most crucial ingredient to any rivalry: the dominant player, Federer. He represented the Goliath in this rivalry, while Rafael Nadal was the up-and-coming star in the international realm of tennis. The young Spaniard played to a slightly younger group of tennis fans. Federer was certainly not old during this period, but Nadal is five years younger, allowing these two to effectively set the stage for a perfect rivalry. Their matches were truly legendary in nature for an entire generation of tennis viewers and the older generation of tennis fans as well.

Novak Djokovic was an up and coming but relatively unknown player during the 2007 season, when Federer faced him twice. Federer's role was thoroughly majestic once again, as he was in the midst of one of his most phenomenal personal seasons in tennis. He had been the reigning champion at each of the Grand Slam majors in 2007 and defeated Rafael Nadal for the second consecutive year at the Wimbledon Final. This year, it had been in stunning fashion, as Nadal had no answer for Federer's dominant serve and resounding final victory. The 2007 US Open in New York City was one of the most memorable performances of his career. Just a few weeks removed from dropping a final match in stunning upset fashion in Montreal against newcomer Djokovic, the sports media lunged at the opportunity to set the stage for a rematch once Federer and Djokovic mowed down the other competition in New York and finally met in a match at the end. This would mark one of Federer's early legendary title defenses, at least according to perceived significance and press coverage. ESPN and other sports media platforms had been fresh off covering Federer's best season as a pro in 2006 and were documenting his continued dominance into the New Year, when the tennis world was shocked by Djokovic in Montreal.

Upon the eve of the Open final, the sports media played up the concept of this rivalry by staging it as another David vs. Goliath scenario. This time, there was a slightly more significant nod to pop-culture as the mainstream press dubbed him "Darth Federer," an ode to the Star Wars pop icon character and Sith Lord. This was also due to Federer having donned an all-black Nike outfit during the competition, and the media certainly played up the concept of this final match being the embodiment of good vs. evil on display for all to witness. This parallel absolutely benefited Federer as the press was mostly jabbing at him in a lighthearted manner. Most of all, it boosted the start of another legendary rivalry with Federer at the center of it all once again, setting the stage for another epic chapter of his illustrious career. The two men would go on to face each other many times, and an incredible spirit of competition existed between the two throughout each of their respective careers.

Ultimately, due to the sheer volume of matches between the two of them within this rivalry (they have played each other 44 times), this rivalry is essentially the most substantial of Federer's career. While Nadal and Federer may have received more media coverage at the time, they played each other a total of ten fewer times. The statistics point to Djokovic as Federer's fiercest competitor. They are the only two male tennis players to have beaten each other in each separate Grand Slam title. While Federer has won four off Djokovic, his counterpart has likewise done the same.

He enjoyed a monster-season statistically in 2006, with 1,674 points. He enjoyed perhaps his most epic run of professional dominance during a three-year stretch leading up to his mammoth statistical output. From 2003 to 2006, Federer compiled a 259–15 record. This run of utter dominance helped cement Federer as a household name, in addition to helping him soar in the minds of tennis buffs. Tennis analysts typically consider whether or not a player absolutely dominated the sport. Both men and women are typically scrutinized heavily when critics discuss their place in the all-time annals of the sport. When a player enjoys a particular run of dominance, such as Bjorn Borg or Serena Williams, critics usually escalate their consideration of that player when it comes to their ranking as one of the all-time legends of the sport. Federer's notoriety continued to expand during this period due to increased coverage of tennis by "The Worldwide Leader in Sports," ESPN. Their style of compiling highlights and quickly palatable bits of information helped make tennis more digestible for the casual fan.

For most of Tiger Woods's superb golf career, ESPN and other infotainment channels helped attract millions of casual viewers to his pursuit of history and Jack Nicklaus, for the simple reason that they could follow developments without actually having to sit down and watch an entire golf event. Hardcore fans of a particular sport will always remain dedicated to spectating live or on television, but the true ascension of a supremely talented athlete in the modern era has been directly correlated to their exposure within pop culture. While hugely popular in the modern world, sports remains a niche subject. The masses within a society will always dictate what is truly popular. Many great players have outstanding careers, while remaining relatively nondescript and unexposed to the general populace. While statistical domination and once-in-a-generation sort of talent certainly helped Federer's exposure, other characteristics such as his aesthetically pleasing demeanor helped make him more marketable from a television standpoint. Particularly in the case of ESPN, stations love to broadcast players and teams that are either good looking or fun to watch. In Federer's case, he benefited from both of these aspects.

This exposure in the sporting world led to Federer's rise as a marketing brand to revere. He is probably most synonymous with his sponsorship from Gillette, the razor company. An extremely large advertiser for at least a decade, Gillette has sponsored athletes like Tiger Woods and Clay Matthews of the Green Bay Packers. Federer capitalized on his international recognition tremendously by accepting the sponsorship and collaborating with Gillette. Due to the massive amount of exposure he received, Federer's face became instantly more recognizable to the general U.S. public. Association plays a huge role in this as well. Prior to Tiger Woods's infidelity scandal, he was among the most trusted brands in all of sports. Nike, Gillette, and other huge American companies employed Woods's endorsement services. Prior to his scandal, it was considered a good thing to be associated with Tiger Woods in most cases, whether in sport or in business.

When many Americans saw the visual of Federer alongside Woods in the many Gillette commercials broadcast near the end of the first decade of the 2000s, many Americans immediately equated him with winning. This visualization of Federer as a winner would further enhance his reputation as an outstanding athlete. Woods was huge internationally, so it also helped escalate Federer's status internationally, a stock which was already very high. All of this exposure, particularly from about 2005 to 2012, which was the heart of his Gillette ad campaigns, also helped play a role in the drama of his rivalry with Rafael Nadal.

By the time Nadal became a serious challenger to Federer's reign as the best male tennis player in the world, many people already saw Federer as just that: the best in the world at his craft. Nadal did of course become a serious threat eventually, but as in all rivalries, their first few competitive meetings featured Federer as the overwhelming favorite and Nadal as the underdog. This also worked in Nadal's favor when he was eventually able to overcome Federer's talent and began winning some of the majors in which they met. Federer's reputation as one of the best of all time, worked to escalate Nadal's reputation internationally and within America as well. Casual fans, who had been introduced to tennis as a viable viewing option because of Federer v. Nadal, were captivated even more when Nadal was able to overcome the challenge of defeating the legendary Federer. It helped even more in the end, as Federer is still competing at a very high level to this day.

In 2015, Federer maintained the world number 3 ranking in Men's tennis, coming in behind Novak Djokovic from Serbia and the English Andy Murray. Nadal ranked as the fifth best Men's player in the tennis rankings in 2015. Djokovic also had a prolific rivalry with Federer, several years after the peak of his rivalry with Nadal. While this rivalry was far less publicized, it still had an impact on keeping Federer current and engaged with the international sports community, as well as in America.

Chapter 5: At Home: The Personal Life of Roger Federer

Roger Federer has taken many significant steps during the course of his tennis career, but when Federer met his future wife at the Sydney Olympic games, he took the most significant and meaningful step in his personal life. The couple now have four children together: two separate sets of twins. His wife, Mirka Vavrinec, was also a tennis player and established herself well internationally.

An excellent, 2014 profile piece done by the Daily Mail in the United Kingdom provides an interesting bit of insight into their marriage and depicts the couple as tennis royalty. While his wife did not have an individually outstanding tennis career (as compared to rival Federer's impact on the game), they are revered in many circles as the "President" and "First Lady" of the sport. The piece details how their marriage revolves around the culture of tennis and just how revered Federer is among those closely associated with the sport. In the piece, Mirka is quoted with regard to how their marriage works so well. "That's why we get along so perfectly. No other woman could deal with so much tennis. If he wants to sleep long, I definitely won't wake him by getting up early." This quote is incredibly revealing into the mindset of perhaps the greatest tennis player of all time and the woman he has chosen as his life partner. It pulls back the curtain on just how dedicated Federer is to the sport of tennis, to even inspire his wife to deliver a quote so intimate.

Apart from the obvious impact his wife and children have had on his lifestyle, his youth trainer, Peter Carter may have had the most instrumentally critical impact on Federer's life. A former tennis player himself, Carter developed the young player's style and technique. By one account, Federer spent more time around Carter than he did his own family for several years during his early teenage years. While he was morphing into a full-time student of the game, Carter was shaping the refinements in his game. Carter was also apparently able to solve a major issue stunting Federer's early growth as a player: his anger. Federer became known by his family and peers to have an extreme temper during a tennis match or some other type of competition. Carter reached Roger in a way no one had yet been able to and convinced him to cut back on his rage during games because his lapses of composure cost him too much energy, which he needed in order to deliver a better performance as a player. Prior to Federer turning professional, Carter united with Peter Lundgren, another trainer, and during this time period, the two men worked to constantly strengthen Federer's game and improve upon any weaknesses he may have had at the time. Carter and Lundgren both ended up playing a huge role within the framework of Federer's life.

In 2002, tragic news struck close to his heart, Peter Carter was killed in a vehicular accident while he was traveling in South Africa. The news struck Roger very hard. Carter had become a real-life mentor to him and he had committed so much of his time to Roger's own improvement. He gave him so much advice about his game, both physically and mentally, which he surely required. He most likely would not have reached such phenomenal heights if he had not had the type of quality instruction he received from Carter. Federer turned 21 just a few days after learning of Carter's death. While the news left Federer in shock, it may have actually had a profound impact on the way he has conducted his life since. Not that he had ever evidently neglected the personal relationships in his life, but the perspective he likely gained from the fragility of life must have changed his perspective in some way.

Chapter 6: Making a Tremendous Impact: Roger's Emotional Connection with Philanthropy

Roger Federer was incredibly inspired by some of the people he encountered in his many travels to Africa. He has spent much of his adult life and spare time trying to do good for others since his ascension to fame. With the blessing of riches comes a choice. People who become famous in the athletic world, music industry, or any other prominent industry within the public sphere always must decide between keeping their wealth completely to themselves or sharing it with the world in order to make it a better place.

Improving the quality of education for children, in particular, struck a chord with Roger. He founded the Roger Federer Foundation with a mission to improve all aspects of the education system for children, typically aged 3 to 17. Likely out of respect for his mother's homeland of South Africa, Federer has placed a large emphasis of his organization's work on improving the quality of a typical South African child's education. His organization's most prominent work takes place in the form of programs across six different southern African nations, including South Africa. Of course, Federer's foundation also places an emphasis on improving the quality of educational resources and the supply of necessities to Swiss children, typically aged 3 to 12, according to the foundation's mission statement.

Federer's philanthropic work furthers the positive perception many people in the public sphere have of him. Many famous athletes and other prominent public figures engage in philanthropic work for various reasons. The dedication it appears he has to ensuring it is successful and that it has an actual impact on the children it aims to help, is reassuring. Many celebrities seem to engage in charity work simply for the publicity, but also seem rather detached. In Federer's case, he absolutely receives some public recognition for his charitable work, but he also appears to be heavily involved and instrumental in its success.

Federer's foundation emphasizes the importance for a clear agenda and they have many ongoing projects. In Switzerland, for example, their mission is to focus on extra-curricular education and instruction, while their southern African goals seem to focus on fundamentals and the improvement of basic education. It certainly seems as if they are dedicated to making a difference and that he truly cares deeply about the education problems these parts of the world face annually.

Roger has become involved in many causes which he feels personally connected to. Upon visiting an audience of thrilled Ethiopian children at a school supported by his foundation in 2010, he was emotionally moved in a significant way by the uproarious greeting he received. This sort of "hands-on" involvement in his charitable work, particularly later in his career, has also helped to define philanthropic meaning in Roger's life. While he could just as easily remain entirely "hands-off" and still maintain an excellent public reputation simply based on the merit of his financial commitment to his charity, he has made it a point to learn about charitable work and experience the results of his giving firsthand.

He also undoubtedly feels an emotional connection the continent of Africa because of his mother's origins in South Africa. Despite clashing with Nadal 34 times over the course of their careers, perhaps the greatest mutual achievement of each man can be measured by their mutually charitable efforts. The Match for Africa was a charitable event organized by the Roger Federer Foundation and designated for the purpose of fulfilling the organization's mission to enhance the school systems and otherwise general quality of life for children in primarily southern African countries. The event was a two-part feature held in Zurich, Switzerland, initially, and took place during an interesting period in each of Federer and Nadal's respective careers. It occurred while Nadal was ranked number one in the world over Federer, so the friendly match featured Roger as the technical underdog at his own organization's charity event. Of course, this event was not about tennis or competitive spirit, but to come together and raise funds for a noble cause. More than 10,000 tickets were sold very quickly and the charity event was a resounding success. Federer won the match in his home country. The second part of this event was held in Nadal's home region of Madrid, Spain. This time, the host was victorious as well. Not that these friendly matches were significant within the grand scheme of who won and who lost, it is simply an interesting glimpse inside the relationship of Federer and Nadal. The true winners in this event were those helped by Federer's foundation. The matches reportedly raised a very significant amount of money. According to crunchsports.com, the Zurich match raised approximately $2.5 million, while the contest in Madrid raised over $1.3 million: a resounding victory for the purpose of charitable work within each of their lives.

Chapter 7: Federer's Tennis Legacy

The example of the model athlete comes around occasionally in our lifetimes. While many sports figures have had an instrumental impact on the nature of the game which made them famous, and they in turn helped to make more famous, very few can claim a career as extraordinary as that of Roger Federer. From A to Z, Federer covered all of the bases as an elite athlete at the relatively young age of 34. Only in the realm of sports do we consider men and women in their 30s to be getting old—perhaps even too old to remain as competitive as they once were in their 20s. Many of the same rules of thumb can be applied across sports. NHL legends Mario Lemieux and Wayne Gretzky, widely recognized as the finest the sport had to historically offer, each had their best statistical seasons before the age of 30.

In the case of Roger Federer, a parallel can immediately be drawn. The fact that he has not won a Grand Slam title since 2012 would cause an analyst to exercise caution before declaring Federer a currently dominant athlete. However, his high ranking and the quality of matches he has continued to win (although no title victories) since 2012 should display that he is still a phenomenal talent to this day and very capable of winning big matches, despite his advanced age. Defining his legacy as a tennis player becomes much more simplified by the fact that he has won the most major championships ever.

Analyzing his place in history would be much more nuanced and difficult were he currently tied with another player for the most all-time titles. However, when someone excels at a sport so extraordinarily as to have won each of the four most significant titles in the sport, and three of them multiple times, it solidifies their grasp on the status of being considered a legend. Another fact to consider is that Federer owns a three-title lead on the all-time record. Pete Sampras and Nadal share second place with 14 victories each. To better put Federer's accomplishments into perspective, he personally has one less major title than Bjorn Borg and John McEnroe, combined. Borg owns 11 titles while McEnroe won 7 over the course of his career. The fact that Federer is just one title removed from these two tennis legends combined goes to show how significant Roger Federer's tennis legacy is.

About the Author

Benjamin Southerland is a lifelong Chicagoland resident. Southerland developed a strong interest for politics and government during his college years through his study of leaders who have shaped history, such as Winston Churchill, Napoleon, and Thomas Jefferson. Southerland is also interested in individuals who have impacted the world of sports and entertainment. He has studied and written about politicians, world leaders, athletes, and celebrities. He researches these fascinating figures extensively in order to determine what has shaped their worldviews and contributed to their success. He aims for his books to give readers a deep understanding of the achievements, inspirations, and goals of the world's most influential individuals. Follow Benjamin Southerland at his website benjaminsoutherland.com to learn about his latest books.